Chris~~tmas~~ JOKE BOOK
Stocking Stuffer

Over 180+ Funny Riddles, Puns, Would You Rather Games, Knock Knock Jokes, Fill-in-The Blank Jokes and More for Kids to Enjoy!

FOR KIDS AGES 6-12

T. WILSON

Copyright ©2024 All rights reserved

No part of this publication may be reproduced, distributed or transmitted, in any form or by any means, including photocopying, recording or other electronic or mechanical methods, without the prior written permission of the publisher, except in the case of brief quotations embodied in reviews and certain other non commercial uses permitted by copyright law.

Contents

This book features:

Christmas Jokes

Christmas Puns

Christmas Riddles

Silly Tongue Twisters

Would You Rather Questions

Fill in The Blank Jokes

Knock Knock Jokes

Funny and Silly Christmas Rhymes

 # Welcome

Welcome, young jokesters, to a magical world of giggles, groans, and guffaws! This special book is packed with Christmas jokes, puns, and riddles, fill in the blank jokes and more that are sure to light up your holiday season with laughter.

Whether you're snuggled up by the fire, sipping on hot cocoa, or decorating the Christmas tree, these jokes will bring a smile to your face and joy to everyone around you.

From Santa's silly antics to Rudolph's reindeer games, you'll find a festive collection of jokes that will make your holiday even brighter!

So, gather your family, invite your friends, and get ready to share the gift of laughter. Remember, the more you laugh, the merrier your Christmas will be!

Are you ready to sleigh them with your best jokes?

Let's get started!

Christmas Jokes

1: Why did Santa go to music school?
He wanted to improve his wrapping skills!

2: What do you get when you cross a snowman and a dog?
Frostbite!

3: Why are Christmas trees so bad at sewing?
They always drop their needles!

4: What's Santa's favorite type of music?
Wrap music!

5: What's a snowman's favorite snack?
Ice Krispies treats!

6: What do you call an old snowman?
Water!

7: What does Santa suffer from if he gets stuck in a chimney?
Claus-trophobia!

8: What kind of photos do elves take?
Elfies!

9: Why did the Christmas tree go to the barber?
It needed a trim!

10: What do you get if you cross an apple with a Christmas tree?
A pineapple!

11: What did one snowman say to the other snowman?
"Do you smell carrots?"

12: Why did the gingerbread man go to school?
He wanted to be a smart cookie!

13: What do snowmen do on Christmas?
They chill out!

14: What do you get if you eat Christmas decorations?
Tinsel-itis!

15: What do you call Santa when he stops moving?
Santa Pause!

16: What do you call Santa when he loses his hat?
You can always sense his presents!

17: Why was the Christmas math book sad?
It had too many problems!

18: What does Rudolph want for Christmas?
A reincheck!

19: What's Santa's favorite type of candy?
Jolly Ranchers!

20: Why don't you ever see Santa in the hospital?
Because he has private elf care!

21: Why did the Christmas tree refuse to leave?
It had too many roots!

22: What do you call a greedy elf?
Elfish!

23: What do Santa's elves use to take pictures?
A "North Pole-aroid" camera!

24: Why did the snowman stand in the middle of the garden?
He wanted to chill with the vegetables!

25: What does Santa do when his elves misbehave?
He gives them the sack!

Christmas Puns

26: What do you call a snowman with a six-pack?
An abdominal snowman!

27: How does Santa keep track of all the fireplaces he's visited?
He keeps a log!

28: What do you call a bunch of chess players bragging about their games in a hotel lobby?
Chess nuts boasting in an open foyer!

29: What do you call an elf who sings?
A wrapper!

30: How does Santa stay in shape?
He sleighs all day!

31: **What do you get if you cross Santa with a detective?**
Santa Clues!

32: **Why did the elf sleep under the Christmas tree?**
Because he wanted to wake up with presents!

33: **What do snowmen like to do on the weekend?**
Chill out!

34: **What's Santa's favorite sandwich?**
Peanut butter and jolly!

35: **What's a Christmas tree's favorite candy?**
Orna-mints!

36: **How do you scare a snowman?**
Point a hairdryer at him!

37: **Why did Santa put a clock in his sleigh?**
He wanted to go back in time!

38: **What do you call a snowman's dog?**
A slush puppy!

39: **What's the difference between a snowman and a snowwoman?**
Snowballs!

40: **What do elves use to take notes in school?**
A "pencil-cane!"

41: **What do you get when you combine a Christmas tree with an iPad?**
A pine-apple!

42: What do you get if you cross a bell with a skunk?
Jingle smells!

43: Why don't snowmen wear shoes?
Because they have cold feet!

44: How do sheep wish each other Merry Christmas?
Fleece Navidad!

45: What kind of motorcycle does Santa ride?
A "Holly-Davidson"!

46: Why was the snowman embarrassed?
He saw the carrot at the bottom of the pool!

47: What do you call a cat on the beach at Christmas?
Sandy Claws!

48: What do you call Santa when he takes a break?
Santa Pause!

49: How do you help someone who's lost their Christmas spirit?
Nurse them back to elf!

50: What do you call a kid who doesn't believe in Santa?
A rebel without a Claus!

Christmas Riddles

51: **Why do mummies like Christmas so much?**
Because of all the wrapping!

52: **What do you call a snowman on rollerblades?**
A snowmobile!

53: **How do elves get to the top floor of the workshop?**
They take the elf-evator!

54: **What did the reindeer say to the elf?**
"Nothing. Reindeer can't talk!"

55: **Why does Santa always enter through the chimney?**
Because it soots him!

56: What do you call Frosty the Snowman in May?
A puddle!

57: How does a Christmas tree keep itself safe?
It wears a tree-sure belt!

58: Why did the reindeer get a divorce?
It was always playing reindeer games!

59: Why did Rudolph get a bad grade in music class?
Because he went down in history!

60: Why was the snowman looking through the carrots?
He was picking his nose!

61: **What do elves learn in school?**
The elf-abet!

62: **What kind of bread does Santa make his sandwiches with?**
"Ho-Ho-Hole-wheat!"

63: **What do you call a broke Santa Claus?**
Saint Nickel-less!

64: **What does Santa do with fat elves?**
He sends them to an elf farm!

65: **Why is Santa so good at karate?**
Because he has a black belt!

66: **How do snowmen travel around?**
By riding an "icicle!"

67: **Why does Santa like to garden?**
Because he loves to watch things "grow-ho-ho!"

68: **What's a snowman's favorite drink?**
Ice tea!

69: **Why did the elf go to school?**
To improve his elf-esteem!

70: **What does a snowman take when it gets sick?**
A chill pill!

71: **What's Santa's favorite cereal?**
Frosted Flakes!

72: **What kind of ball doesn't bounce?**
A snowball!

73: **What do you call a reindeer ghost?**
Cariboo!

74: **What does Santa use to clean his sleigh?**
Comet!

75: **What do reindeer say before they tell a joke?**
This one's gonna sleigh you!

76: **What did one Christmas tree say to the other?**
Lighten up!

77: **What do you call a kid who won't help decorate the Christmas tree?**
The Grinch!

78: **What does Santa grow in his garden?**
Christmas peas!

79: **What do you call an elf who won't share?**
Elfish!

80: **What is a Christmas tree's favorite candy?**
Orna-mints!

81: Why don't snowmen get angry?
They just let it go!

82: Why was the elf late to work?
He had to catch the Gingerbread Express!

83: Why did Santa go to the beach?
He wanted to catch some rays!

84: What do snowmen eat for breakfast?
Frosted Flakes!

85: What's a reindeer's favorite game?
Freeze tag!

86: **What's an elf's favorite sport?**
North Pole vaulting!

87: **What do you call a snowman party?**
A snowball!

88: **How do you fix a broken Christmas tree?**
With tree-sin!

89: **What do you call a dinosaur at Christmas?**
A Christmasaurus!

90: **Why don't snowmen wear scarves?**
Because they have snow necks!

91: **What did Santa say to the smoker?**
Please don't smoke, it's bad for my "elf!"

92: **How does Santa clean his suit?**
He uses Santa-tizer!

93: **What does Santa use to bake cookies?**
Elf-raising flour!

94: **Why was the gingerbread man so cool?**
He knew how to roll with it!

95: **How does Santa take care of sick elves?**
He nurses them back to elf!

96: Why was the snowman so happy?
He heard the snow blower was coming!

97: What did the reindeer say to the elf when he got too close?
Back off, bucko!

98: What do snowmen wear on their heads?
Ice caps!

99: What does Santa give to naughty boys and girls?
Coal!

100: Why does Santa go down chimneys?
Because they soot him!

Silly Tongue Twisters

Try saying this five times fast...

1: Santa's Sleigh Swiftly Soars Southward

Try saying this five times fast...

2: Elves Elegantly Embellish Enormous Evergreen Trees

Try saying this five times fast...

3: Rudolph Races Rapidly Around Rooftops

Try saying this five times fast...

4: Frosty's Frosty Feet Freeze Fast

Try saying this five times fast...

5: Giggling Gingerbread Men Gallop Gleefully

Try saying this five times fast...

~~[redacted]~~

6: Cheerful Children Chase Colorful Candy Canes

Try saying this five times fast...

7: Silly Santa Sings Sweet Seasonal Songs

Try saying this five times fast...

8: Jolly Jingle Bells Jingle Joyfully

Try saying this five times fast...

9: Busy Baking Elves Balance Big Batches

Try saying this five times fast...

10: Bright bells bring big bundles of bouncing bows

Would You Rather Questions

Would You Rather..

Have a glowing red nose like Rudolph or pointy ears like an elf?

Get presents every day in December or one huge present on Christmas Day?

Build a snowman or have a snowball fight?

Would You Rather..

Eat only candy canes or only Christmas cookies for a week?

Ride in Santa's sleigh or help in his workshop?

Sing Christmas carols all day or wear a Santa hat for a week?

Would You Rather..

Open your presents on Christmas Eve or Christmas morning?

Drink hot cocoa or apple cider on a snowy day

Decorate the Christmas tree or bake Christmas cookies?

Be a reindeer or an elf?

Would You Rather..

Make ornaments for the Christmas tree or string popcorn to decorate it?

Have a pet reindeer or a pet snowman?

Spend a day as Santa or as one of his reindeer?

Would You Rather..

Have a Christmas party with your friends or a quiet day with your family?

Wear reindeer antlers or Santa's hat all day?

Listen to only one Christmas song all season or watch only one Christmas movie?

Would You Rather..

Have Santa's beard or Frosty's hat?

Visit a Christmas market or a Christmas tree farm?

Help wrap gifts or help bake Christmas cookies?

Would You Rather..

Live in a world where it's always Christmas or never Christmas?

Have a talking Christmas tree or a flying snowman?

Find a candy cane forest or a gingerbread village?

Would You Rather..

Have to wear a full Santa suit for a day or elf shoes for a week?

Visit Santa's workshop or his stables?

Decorate 100 Christmas cookies or 100 Christmas ornaments?

Would You Rather..

Write a Christmas card to Santa or receive one from him?

Spend Christmas in a cabin in the snowy woods or on a warm beach?

Get a stocking full of small toys or one big present?

Would You Rather..

Have a Christmas tree that never loses its needles or Christmas lights that never burn out?

Would you rather build the biggest snowman ever or light up the brightest house on the block?

Create your own Christmas movie or direct a Christmas play for school?

Fill-in-the-Blank Jokes

Fill in the blanks with your own funny words to create silly and unique Christmas jokes! Let your imagination run wild!

Cool Christmas Outfit

1: Why did the _____ wear a _____?

Answer: To look cool at the Christmas party!

Fill in the blanks with your own funny words to create silly and unique Christmas jokes! Let your imagination run wild!

Santa's Big Surprise

2: What did Santa say when he saw the _____?

Answer: That's one _____ Christmas!"

Fill in the blanks with your own funny words to create silly and unique Christmas jokes! Let your imagination run wild!

Sleigh Ride to the North Pole

3: How did the _____ get to the North Pole?

Answer: He took a _____!

Fill in the blanks with your own funny words to create silly and unique Christmas jokes! Let your imagination run wild!

Hungry Reindeer

4: Why did the reindeer eat the _____?

Answer: Because it was feeling _____!

Fill in the blanks with your own funny words to create silly and unique Christmas jokes! Let your imagination run wild!

Elf's Funny Comment

5: What did the elf say to the _____?

Answer: I've never seen a _____ Christmas like this!

Fill in the blanks with your own funny words to create silly and unique Christmas jokes! Let your imagination run wild!

Snowman's Winter Adventure

6: How did the snowman end up in the _____?

Answer: He slipped on a _____!

Fill in the blanks with your own funny words to create silly and unique Christmas jokes! Let your imagination run wild!

Gingerbread Man's Day Out:

~~~~~~~~~~~~

7: Why did the gingerbread man go to the _____?

Answer: To get a _____!

Fill in the blanks with your own funny words to create silly and unique Christmas jokes! Let your imagination run wild!

Mrs. Claus's Surprise

8: What did Mrs. Claus say when she saw the _____?

Answer: That's a _____ surprise!

Fill in the blanks with your own funny words to create silly and unique Christmas jokes! Let your imagination run wild!

Christmas Tree's Reaction

9: How did the Christmas tree feel after the _____?

Answer: A little _____!

Fill in the blanks with your own funny words to create silly and unique Christmas jokes! Let your imagination run wild!

Christmas Eve Adventure

10: Why did the _____ cross the road on Christmas Eve?

Answer: To get to the _____!

Fill in the blanks with your own funny words to create silly and unique Christmas jokes! Let your imagination run wild!

The Climbing Christmas Tree

11: Why did the _____ climb up the Christmas tree?

Answer: Because it wanted to _____ from the top!

Fill in the blanks with your own funny words to create silly and unique Christmas jokes! Let your imagination run wild!

Santa's Workshop Surprise

12: What did Santa say when he found a _____ in his workshop

Answer: This is _____ unbelievable!

Fill in the blanks with your own funny words to create silly and unique Christmas jokes! Let your imagination run wild!

Reindeer Decorations

13: How did the reindeer decorate the _____?

Answer: With lots of _____ and a big shiny _____ on top!

Fill in the blanks with your own funny words to create silly and unique Christmas jokes! Let your imagination run wild!

Tangled in Lights

14: Why did the _____ get tangled in the Christmas lights?

Answer: Because it was trying to _____ its way out of the _____!

Fill in the blanks with your own funny words to create silly and unique Christmas jokes! Let your imagination run wild!

Christmas Fanatic

~~~~~~~~~~~~~

15: What do you call a _____ that loves Christmas?

Answer: A _____ fanatic!

Fill in the blanks with your own funny words to create silly and unique Christmas jokes! Let your imagination run wild!

Snowman Style

16: Why did the snowman put a _____ on its head?

Answer: Because it wanted to feel _____ and _____!

Fill in the blanks with your own funny words to create silly and unique Christmas jokes! Let your imagination run wild!

Elf's Big Discovery

17: What did the elf say when it saw a giant _____?

Answer: I've never seen a _____ that big!

Fill in the blanks with your own funny words to create silly and unique Christmas jokes! Let your imagination run wild!

Gingerbread Fixer-Upper

18: How did the gingerbread man fix his broken _____?

Answer: With some _____ and a lot of _____!

Fill in the blanks with your own funny words to create silly and unique Christmas jokes! Let your imagination run wild!

Mrs. Claus's Secret Recipe

19: What did Mrs. Claus bake with the extra _____?

Answer: A batch of _____ flavored cookies!

Fill in the blanks with your own funny words to create silly and unique Christmas jokes! Let your imagination run wild!

The Busy _____:

20: Why did the _____ refuse to help Santa?

Answer: Because it was too busy _____ in the _____!

Knock Knock Jokes

Have fun with these knock knock jokes!

1: Knock, knock.
Who's there?
Snow.
Snow who?
Snow business like show business!

Have fun with these knock knock jokes!

2: Knock, knock.
Who's there?
Holly.
Holly who?
Holly-days are here again!

Have fun with these knock knock jokes!

3: Knock, knock.
Who's there?
Ice.
Ice who?
Ice to meet you,
Merry Christmas!

Have fun with these knock knock jokes!

4: Knock, knock.
Who's there?
Snowman.
Snowman who?
Snowman, no cry!

Have fun with these knock knock jokes!

5: Knock, knock.
Who's there?
Candy.
Candy who?
Candy cane come out to play?

Have fun with these knock knock jokes!

6: Knock, knock.
Who's there?
Merry.
Merry who?
Merry Christmas and a Happy New Year!

Have fun with these knock knock jokes!

7: Knock, knock.
Who's there?
Olive.
Olive who?
Olive the other reindeer!

Have fun with these knock knock jokes!

8: Knock, knock.
Who's there?
Rudolph.
Rudolph who?
Rudolph the red-nosed reindeer!

Have fun with these knock knock jokes!

9: Knock, knock.
Who's there?
Elf.
Elf who?
Elf you clean up, Santa will be here soon!

Have fun with these knock knock jokes!

10: Knock, knock.
Who's there?
Jingle.
Jingle who?
Jingle all the way to the door!

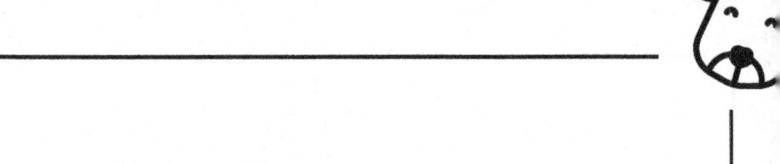

Have fun with these knock knock jokes!

11: Knock, knock.
Who's there?
Santa.
Santa who?
Santa Claus is coming to town!

Have fun with these knock knock jokes!

12: Knock, knock.
Who's there?
Bells.
Bells who?
Bells on bobtail ring!

Have fun with these knock knock jokes!

13: Knock, knock.
Who's there?
Tinsel.
Tinsel who?
Tinsel time for Christmas!

Have fun with these knock knock jokes!

14: Knock, knock.
Who's there?
Tree.
Tree who?
Tree-mendous things are happening this Christmas!

Have fun with these knock knock jokes!

15: Knock, knock.
Who's there?
Noel.
Noel who?
Noel, Noel, the first Noel!

Have fun with these knock knock jokes!

16: Knock, knock.
Who's there?
Fleece.
Fleece who?
Fleece Navidad!

Have fun with these knock knock jokes!

17: Knock, knock. Who's there? Snowflake. Snowflake who? Snowflake, the winter wonderland!

Have fun with these knock knock jokes!

18: Knock, knock.
Who's there?
Stocking.
Stocking who?
Stocking up on Christmas cheer!

Have fun with these knock knock jokes!

19: Knock, knock.
Who's there?
Ginger.
Ginger who?
Gingerbread man, let me in!

Have fun with these knock knock jokes!

20: Knock, knock.
Who's there?
Frosty.
Frosty who?
Frosty the snowman!

Funny and Silly Christmas Rhymes

Santa's Lost Boot

Santa lost a boot in the snow so deep,

Now he's hopping around, trying not to slip!

But don't worry, kids, there's nothing to fear,

He'll bring all the gifts with a frosty foot here!

Reindeer Games

Rudolph played a game of tag,

Dasher said, "You're it, don't lag!"

But when Rudolph tried to hide,

His nose lit up the whole hillside!

Elf on the Shelf

The elf on the shelf is watching all night,

But when the lights go out, he's out of sight!

He dances and pranks till the morning sun,

Then back to his spot, pretending he's done!

Gingerbread Man's Escape

The gingerbread man ran out the door,

Saying, "Catch me if you can, like before!"

But then it rained, and he got all wet,

Now he's just a crumbly, soggy pet!

Christmas Tree Trouble

The Christmas tree wobbled and started to sway,

"Who hung all this tinsel?" it started to say.

But before it could topple and fall on the floor,

The cat ran right through it and out the door!

Frosty's Dance

Frosty the snowman tried to dance,

But he tripped on his hat and lost his chance!

His carrot nose wiggled, his buttons flew high,

Now he's rolling downhill, waving goodbye!

Santa's Snack

Santa took a bite of a cookie so sweet,

Then hopped back in his sleigh, ready to fleet.

But the cookie was big and got stuck in his beard,

Now he's off to the next house looking a bit weird!

Reindeer Antics

The reindeer were playing in Santa's sleigh,

When Dasher dared Dancer to fly away.

They zoomed through the sky, did loops and a flip,

And Santa just sighed, "Please don't let us tip!"

The Sneaky Elf

An elf sneaked a candy cane from the tree,

And giggled, "This treat is just for me!"

But then Santa caught him, quick as a wink,

Now the elf's on the naughty list—what do you think?

Jingle Bells Mix-Up

Jingle bells, jingle bells, jingle all the way,

But the bells were too loud and scared Santa's sleigh!

The reindeer jumped and ran out of sight,

Now Santa's chasing them through the night!

Thank You For Your Purchase!

Thank you so much for purchasing my Christmas joke, riddle, and activity book for kids!

I hope it fills your holiday season with laughter and fun. Your support truly means the world to me, and I'm so grateful to have you as part of this creative journey.

If you and your little ones enjoyed the jokes and activities, I'd love to hear your thoughts! Leaving a review helps me keep the magic going and share it with even more families.

Wishing you a joyful and festive holiday season! And don't forget to check out my other books available on Amazon under T. Wilson—I'd love for you to explore more of what I've created.

Warmest wishes,
T. Wilson

Made in United States
North Haven, CT
12 December 2024

62342135R00059